Gunmetal Sky

by

Howie Good

Gunmetal Sky

Copyright © 2021 Howie Good

All rights reserved.

No part of this publication may be reproduced, distributed, or transmitted in any form or by any means, including photocopying, recording, or other electronic or mechanical methods, without the prior written permission of the publisher, except in brief quotations embodied in critical reviews, citations, and literary journals for noncommercial uses permitted by copyright law.

ISBN-13: 978-1-7345158-5-5

Cover design by Josh Dale

Author photo by Howie Good

Printed in the U.S.A.

For more titles and inquiries, please visit:

www.thirtywestph.com

Table of Contents

Beginner's Guide to Dystopia 11
People Get Ready 12
'Grief Is Love Made Homeless' 13
The Trouble with Being Born 14
Flash Bang Boom 15
Culture Wars 16
War Baby 17
Chaos Theory 18
The Gray Man 19
A Toast to the Dark 20
The Speech Police 21
American Tune 22
Dream Interpretation 23
Complicity 24
In Case of Fire 25
Love in Time of 26
The Secret Goldfish 27
Love Note 28
Dust and Bones 29
The Third Reich of Dreams 30
Without a Map 31
The Carnival of Being 32
Premonitory Signs of Decay 33
Safety Instructions for the Twenty-First Century 34
Heartsick 35

A New Kind of Heaven	36
April Come She Will	37
Echo's Bones	38
Tunnel Vision	39
Advice for the Perplexed	40
Repairing the World	41
Do-It-Yourself Destruction	42
White Privilege	43
A Town Called Nowhere	44
Chili Con Carnage	45
Flurries	49
Holocaust Train	50
Cold Sun	51
On Being Rendered Speechless	52
A Simple Prayer	53
Who Is a Righteous Man?	54
Statistic	55
The Day's Residue	59
Half-Mumbled Sentences	60
After the Bomb	61
Only Beauty Survives	62
Life and Nothing But	63
It's Not Me, It's You	64
Oh, Mercy	65
Rotten Tomatoes	66
Eve of the Eve of Destruction	67
Heart on Ice	68
After Auschwitz	69
The Ladder	70

Apathy for the Devil 71
Birth, Death, Etc. 72
Threatened Birds Nesting 73
Pandemic 74
Connotations of Ancestral Home 75
After the Plague 76
Epistemologies of Ignorance 77
The End of Nature 78
Anniversary 79
Oracle 80
Flight into Darkness 81
Sick World 82
Between Life and Death 83
The Endless Inventory of Human Cruelty 84
Stick Figure Family 85
Failed Poet Theater 86
Anger Is an Arrow 87
Mood Pill 88
For Those Who Are Ignorant of History 89
Do the Paranoid Style 90
Gunmetal Sky 91
Acknowledgements & Citations 92
About the Author 93

You cannot change humanity; you can only know it.

—Gustave Flaubert

I

Beginner's Guide to Dystopia

From the street outside, a loudspeaker boomed: "According to the decree of the 17th of this month on the Abolition of Walls..." I got up from the table where I was reading and went to the window. Banners with the slogan "Public Interest Comes Before Self-Interest" fluttered in endless repetition down the street. Practically right under my window, officers were clubbing a man lying crumpled on the pavement. I sighed, then sat back down and found my place in my book. Sea nymphs with red seaweed hair were sunning themselves on the ledges of seaside cliffs.

People Get Ready

Any one of us is every one of us, if you get what I mean. I want to tap this guy and that guy and that woman on the shoulder and tell them all, "You can't be lost in your own world all the time." But, of course, I won't. The train is approaching the station, and the degree of courage required to board keeps multiplying. I look at the gray faces of the other travelers skulking about the platform. If they only knew that the same gene that gives birds the ability to sing gives us the ability to speak!

'Grief Is Love Made Homeless'

I was born shivering in a small Midwestern city named for a now-extinct tribe. As I grew older, I was given platitudes to speak and warned not to mix up the words or mistake their meaning. Occasionally, the sky would brighten, but never for long, and then people would cluster on street corners and in churches and under highway bridges. Some would be crying, having just learned that being guilty was a part of life. This happened again and again and again. It might have been more endurable if the dark wasn't always so dark.

The Trouble with Being Born

The birds that visited my feeder last winter scattered sunflower seeds that are just beginning, somewhat triumphantly, to sprout. I smiled to myself when I found them today at the very back of the garden, poking up like little periscopes, but still blind to every danger.

&

When I see someone walking toward me, I try to be invisible. You just don't know the threat they may pose. Are they contagious? Are they drunk or on drugs? Do they have a concealed weapon? What's funny, though, is that if I traced my ancestry back far enough, I would probably discover I am everyone's cousin.

&

I always had doubts. Then, in 1996, three members of my family got cancer. In my dream, I dig them up, spray them down with concoctions, and then let them bake and dry and rot in the sun. Horror is everywhere. Lock your doors, lady.

Flash Bang Boom

With the encouragement of family and friends, I adopted a retired bomb-sniffing dog. I called him Flash—"After the flashing lights of a migraine," I would joke to anyone who asked. One day, he discovered under the couch the severed head of a doll I didn't even know I had. Next, the piano stopped making sounds when I sat down to play it. Then the tree outside my window appeared suspended like an astronaut in space. Now I often catch the dog lying on the couch, studying me with cold, squinty eyes, as if calculating exactly how much a person can bear.

Culture Wars

The landlord was on the phone demanding the rent. There were some crumpled bills and a couple of bucks in change on top of the dresser—enough for cigarettes and scratch-offs, maybe a cheap bottle of red. I quoted the Psalms to him: "Even the sparrow finds a home, and the swallow a nest for herself. . ." The sunset faded as we argued back and forth. An almost-purple black settled over the city. I brought a full container of gasoline with me next time I went out. A passerby who caught a glimpse muttered, "Oh fuck, oh fuck, oh fuck, oh fuck." Roots twisted and bulged beneath the asphalt.

War Baby

A war ends. But what changes? The magician, after all, doesn't actually make the card disappear. On the birthing table, the ghastly queen—legs spread apart, mind full of pus—pushes and pants and pushes again. I'm not marching, but I can hear the chants of protesters. When I go out into the street, the sky that burns at dawn bleeds at dusk. I try to seem like just a regular guy. I call it box, snatch, snapper, muff, beaver, pussy, honey pot, cooch, slit, hoo-haw, but never what it is: the rushing buzzing of everything.

Chaos Theory

I like naps. As it wasn't too late, I wanted to enjoy a nap under a tree. I started for the door, but a short stocky man with an uncanny resemblance to Stalin—the dictator who put the "p" in paranoia—caught me by the arm. Of all those present, only he had a distinct shadow, and he projected it onto walls, ceilings, furniture—anything. "Fishing," he said, "is a metaphor for Alzheimer's." He sounded pissed about it, too. I promised myself right then that, when this was over, I would resolve the things eating away at me.

&

Some days I walk to think, some days to actually get somewhere. I've been thinking about death a lot lately—whether there are flickering emojis at the end, or steel bars on all the windows; whether Jesus appears with the hateful look on his face that my father would give me whenever he hissed, "What are you, stupid?" It's perplexing just how much darkness a person can swallow and still function. Van Gogh, the morning before his suicide, had painted a forest scene full of sun and life.

&

I was anxious about what might happen next now that transvestite vampire biker nuns from outer space were shooting death rays from their fingertips. So I dove into a viscerally beautiful, turbulent place. I was soon wishing I hadn't. There were people there who could recite the four rules for the perfect selfie by heart: hold your phone high; know your angle; know your lighting; no duck face!

&

The beach is deserted this time of year, but the light is particularly beautiful, as if infused with the tenderest feelings for all the bleakness it touches. She gets out her phone to take a picture. I'm standing a slight distance off, the sparkling ocean at my back, waiting for her to tell me when to smile.

The Gray Man

A man covered in gray dust was walking. He was very far away, but he never stopped walking. He was walking to find me. No matter how long it took, he would find his way up the steps to my door. My family was sitting on the couch in front of the TV. I was in the other room. They couldn't hear me. It was as if I was pressed between glass. I felt so lonely. The gray man was walking up the steps to the door, and then knocking on the door, and then pounding, and then trying to push the door in. It's an old story, told over and over and over again. I'm just telling it one more time. We know that something is very wrong, and we are living it.

A Toast to the Dark

My maternal grandparents arrived in America on a ship that was built in the same shipyard as the Titanic. All these years later, white judges in black robes are still pondering who was ultimately responsible. Sometimes they burst into tears, sometimes into laughter. Often they slurp Chivas Regal straight from the bottle. When they do, destroying angels clink glasses.

The Speech Police

What was protocol when I went to sleep may be heresy by the time I wake up. I live in dread of undergoing medieval rites of purification—having, for example, fire applied to the penis and the tip of the tongue. My words once had the force of acts. Now my voice comes out hesitant, muffled. I can almost feel the police hiding nearby, just waiting for me to trip on a forbidden phrase or state an unwelcome opinion. Space and light are shrinking. Where there was the peal of bells, there is only the squeak of history's hinges.

American Tune

Love everything that lives, and be fair to all the parts, and do not have a hierarchy, but should the uniforms come for you under the cover of night to convey you back across the border, resolve to become like the wind that dies one moment only to return the next as poems and explosions.

&

I was driving because she couldn't drive a stick—my window half-open, the air rushing past, *whup-whup-whup*—when suddenly there was a sulfur smell like witches burning. She looked up from her phone screen and saw the dreary sky and then the ramshackle ruins of an abandoned factory behind prison fencing. "Are we lost?" she asked. *Well, yeah, maybe.*

&

We were a block or so from our hotel, holding hands like a couple of teenagers, when we saw the dark, lumpy shape—a homeless person wrapped in a shroud of blankets and sleeping on cardboard—but said nothing about it, quick looked away, and walked past at a picked-up pace, as if a crime had just been committed, and our entire role in it was to forget.

Dream Interpretation

When I jerk awake, it's still dark, my wife deep asleep beside me. I have a terrible stiff neck, and I think I can detect a lingering smell of blood. I had just dreamed that I had been sentenced to death by decapitation for an unspecified crime. The next thing I knew, I was walking through a crowd very gingerly, trying to keep my head balanced on my neck stump. Only two or three people even bothered to scream out. The rest must have been practitioners of the new brutality, unaffected by the sight of blood, indifferent almost.

Complicity

We dance with skeletons. We steal cable. We leave violent stains on the carpet. We shift the blame to the fellaheen digging for papyri at an ancient historical site. We cross off career options. We put likeable liars in office and dark-skinned mothers and babies in jail. We go around looking for this or that clue, this or that miraculous city, without even once catching a glimpse. Rather, where our gaze just happens to fall, worse soon follows. The ground bleeds; the moon aches. Fire chews through brick walls. Ideas lose elasticity. The dreaming heads of sleepers get pried open.

In Case of Fire

The seamstresses bend to the demanding work of sewing mouths shut with curved needles and fire-retardant thread. And why shouldn't they? The only words anyone ever truly needs have all been cannibalized for parts. It's the reason I carry a lot of photos in my phone. Still, if someone announces, "I think I'm going to kill myself," you should take it seriously. I've been lingering for a while now very close to a volcano with a beautiful name.

Love in Time of . . .

The spring has started off all wrong. It's been dark and murky, and I've got no idea why. I'm struggling to keep the screech of panic out of my voice. Chinese! The sky is full of them. I think maybe what I need more than isolation or bleach is the soft, reassuring weight of your body on mine. The grim faces on TV advise completely the opposite, but we're meant to be held by each other, amazed by how much we can touch.

The Secret Goldfish

My mother, during one of her frequent fits, flushed my goldfish down the toilet while I was at school. This was long before children had only the water from toilets to drink. I'd won the goldfish at a carnival by somehow tossing a ping-pong ball into the fish's bowl. But awful sights were creeping up on me even then. I have memories of little ballerinas wearing disintegrating tulle tutus and dance slippers made of bubble wrap and tape. And because I was in the country I was in, there were dim streetlamps at dusk, there were burnt holes for eyes.

Love Note

Even though the sign says, "Do not swim near seals," we'll have fun, go on a picnic in the hills, maybe spend the whole night there, so many stars that the sky looks perforated by cosmic buckshot; or we'll sleep in and then helicopter over traffic jams, moving, breathing, shining from rehab center to wedding cake palace, while the angel of death rolls a cigarette and the border wall sinks another quarter of an inch; and this will happen again and again, people turning up at all hours to complain bitterly about being written out of our story.

Dust and Bones

I was walking across the parking lot at Staples when I saw you through a rain-warped windshield, and my heart leaped, but barely a second later, I realized it couldn't really be you, dead all these years. It was just a woman who kind of resembled you, and as I stepped inside the store to buy an accordion folder (with A–Z tabs), I thought of us and the saltiness of your kisses, and then something like rage followed me along the aisles. By the time I found the folder and paid for it with a card and walked back out, the you-that-wasn't-you was gone.

The Third Reich of Dreams

I dreamed that it was forbidden to dream, but that I did it anyway. In the morning, the phone rang. A dull voice said, "This is the Monitoring Office." I started begging and pleading that this one time I be forgiven: "Please just don't report anything this one time. Don't pass it on. Please just forget it." The voice remained absolutely silent and then hung up. Over the next few days, street signs were replaced on every corner with posters proclaiming, in white letters on a black background, the 20 words people weren't allowed to say. The first was "Lord"; the last was "I."

Without a Map

That country no longer exists. If you ever go searching for it—in books or on old maps—you'll find only a confusion of names. Yesterday I was walking and walking and walking and writing poetry in my head, and when I looked up, I realized I had no idea where I was. You don't believe something like that is ever going to happen to you. And then it does. The world is just so huge that none of us is one hundred percent safe. *Is that vehicle following me?* I find myself wondering. *Are those cameras on that turret trained on me?* Somehow the false expresses what might be real. A hunter thinks he shot a deer when he actually shot his brother.

The Carnival of Being

It's so bleak outside that I decide to hide out for the day in my little room. The other first-floor tenant has removed his clothes and walked off down the street. I can't stop replaying in my head the saddest sound in the world: a shovelful of soil thumping the lid of a coffin. For now, at least, there's no great difference between a funeral and a carnival. Volunteer firefighters have been going around the neighborhood distributing oxygen masks for pets. Asthma sufferers, especially. That's the problem with people who put Velveeta on enchiladas—they can't tell anymore what's appropriate. By evening, white hairs have sprouted on just one side of my moustache.

Premonitory Signs of Decay

So far today it's been the usual—derailments, riots, floods, domestic murders—and now the gods of death and destruction are clustered around the microwave in the break room, smirking at something one of them, the really fat one, has just said.

&

In 1911, Duncan MacDougall—a physician from Haverhill, Massachusetts—attempted to photograph the soul leaving the body. But, after a series of highly publicized experiments involving some dozen terminally-ill patients, Dr. MacDougall was forced to concede that "soul substance" might become too agitated at the moment of death to be photographed. I don't like having my picture taken either.

&

It's a scientific fact: a lot of people get depressed on Sundays, usually starting about 4 o'clock. They feel a kind of inexplicable grief as the afternoon is infiltrated by premonitions of the week to come. "Aren't you scared?" you ask. I'm not entirely immune, if that's what you mean. I crack open a fortune cookie, and there's no fortune inside.

Safety Instructions for the Twenty-First Century

It probably won't look like the real you. Stay calm when you come upon it. Face it and stand upright. Speak firmly to it. Do what you can to appear larger—raise your arms, or open your jacket if you're wearing one. You want to convince it you aren't prey and may, in fact, be a danger to it. Give it a way to escape, but if it attacks, don't panic and run. People have fought it with rocks, sticks, caps, jackets, garden tools, and their bare hands. So remain standing, or at least try to get back up.

Heartsick

The doctor is absurdly talkative. "Apparently it's Mental Health Awareness Day today," he says. "And ski season is coming. I've never been to California, and, yes, that's sad." He keeps up his chattering while jamming a giant needle into my chest. I beg him, "Stop, stop, please stop." He just pushes the needle in deeper. I'm screaming now. A nurse hurries in. "Almost there," the doctor calmly tells her, referring, I imagine in my distress, to the outskirts of heaven, where angels—some the size of a grain of salt, some the size of a pebble—buzz like dung flies.

A New Kind of Heaven

The hangman was drunk on the job. A sheriff's deputy had to climb up to press the button that triggered the trap door. It was 1936 and the last public execution in the United States. A medical student conducted the autopsy. He took out the intestines, said, "Yup, it's all there," and then shoved them back in. The body was buried in a secret location for reasons that have never been satisfactorily explained. Today we go about these things entirely differently. An osprey passes overhead with steady, languid wingbeats while clutching in its claws a fish astonished to be flying.

April Come She Will

Men on the street would call my girlfriend *linda*. "Get used to it," she said. I decided the best thing for me to do was nothing. April had been designated Artichoke Month. I remember we saw a movie about astronauts on a mind-bending journey to the cosmic womb. It was confusing and a little scary. She got really into a singer-songwriter who had committed suicide by stabbing himself in the chest. There were long lines outside liquor stores and gun shops. One day we found a crudely-lettered cardboard sign lying abandoned on the sidewalk: Hungry & Cold / Anything Helps.

Echo's Bones

I'm no psychologist, or any other kind of -ologist, but before you go to bed at night, look at the darkness. We're living a life of shadows, of echoes, and with some particles capable of switching between the two. You don't look like you anymore. I'm not there even when I am. At times I resolve to become like the drunks who, sufficiently enraged, can just shrug off the effects of being tasered. Other times what interests me isn't success, but love—how the next person adds onto it without knowing all its nimble and sinister tricks.

Tunnel Vision

Thinking about escaping across closed borders, I dug a hole outside. It was hard work. As I dug deeper, I pulled out bricks, barbed wire, glass bottles and jars, and old cans. When my mind drifted too far into sadness, I stopped. Everything moves slowly now. I'm learning to be stingy with supplies. On the table is a bunch of flowers I found in the trash. Somehow, just looking at them feels like a hopeful gesture.

Advice for the Perplexed

Wash your sex toys (your unmotorized ones, at any rate) in the top rack of the dishwasher. Have a trick for getting bong water out of the carpet. White wine, ironically, gets out red wine stains. Try to avoid being carried off by a UFO when you can just walk. However long it takes, count all the ways there are to kill a person—hanging, shooting, stabbing, drowning, poisoning, beheading, stoning. . . Make mute despair your default greeting to people you pass on the stairs. And always remember: a wild bull becomes docile if tethered to a fig tree.

Repairing the World

Like in a riot, police were shooting rubber bullets. I was rushed by strangers to the hospital. It was dark, stifling, and dingy. The doctor cut my feet open and put pennies in the incisions before sewing them back up and wrapping them in bandages. We were both crying. The moment had the reverence of a flag-burning ceremony when a flag is too ragged to fly. Later, at home, I looked down and saw the bandages were bloody. My mother said, "I just need to grab a lab coat and one egg and I can fix this."

Do-It-Yourself Destruction

People kept coming into my late parents' apartment to collect stuff. One took away some sort of boat. No one seemed to particularly care if cities were burning. A woman from another floor started stroking my face. I asked her to stop. She wouldn't. Her boyfriend was standing right next to her, but didn't say anything, just watched. A week passed, maybe more. The news was unbearable. Gas grenades and rubber bullets. Chants of "I can't breathe. I can't breathe." First responders climbed the stairs two at a time despite the terrible weight of the unshed tears they were carrying.

White Privilege

If you look out the window, you too might see the horizon line fizzing like a lighted fuse. I haven't slept well since then. We need to have a conversation, decide on a plan—something. Just this morning, I heard frightening noises and pictured a baby with a swastika tattooed on his forehead crawling over corpses, statues being toppled, the blowjob mouth of an inflatable sex doll screaming. Given a choice, I would prefer to live in a peace-loving country, a place kind of like Switzerland, just without all the cows and glaciers.

A Town Called Nowhere

This feels like the wrong place for me to be, then it doesn't, and then it does—something to do, perhaps, with the municipal building melting back into the ground. One guy takes offense at my comments, threatens to cut me up and feed the pieces to his dog. Joggers and parents with strollers point their camera phones at us in anticipation of capturing a fatal beating. No one apparently has a better idea of what to do. I want to tell them it'll be OK, but they would only shake their heads and laugh and keep recording.

Chili Con Carnage

The train was crowded, dirty, excruciatingly slow. I had boarded with the idea of arriving that night in time to be a character in someone else's dreams. It doesn't have to make sense, but, for a while, the train ran parallel to an oily black river in which naked corpses floated. None of the passengers traveling with small children even attempted to shield the children's eyes. And that was fine with me. Growing up, I spent many hours watching TV alone in the basement in the dark.

&

I said to the doctor, "I'm dying." He asked, "How's that my fault?" I had been suffering for about a month. The doctor said it was my body attacking itself. "It'll scald you," he said with unexpected enthusiasm, "peel the skin and muscle right off your bones." I wondered if this was a joke of some sort. I decided it must be and climbed down from the exam table. When I opened the door to leave, a man with a bloody face, his hands bound behind his back, was just standing there waiting his turn.

&

I wake up in bed alone, with drool and sweat and maybe worse on my pillow. History is dead. Scum is all that's left. The sun keeps showing up regardless.

II

Flurries

Small white envelopes
blowing all about,
some torn open
and already empty,
but others with invitations
to a children's party
forever sealed inside.

Holocaust Train

We were put into open train cars
and huddled together to keep warm.

When it snowed, we collected it
to drink, because they didn't give us

water. We were in such complete
solidarity that when one of us fell

asleep standing (there was no room
to sit or lie down) none of the others

would steal the snow that accumulated
on her. That snow belonged to her.

Cold Sun

Every day, the world
burns down anew
on the six o'clock news.

A window shimmering
with streaming raindrops
moves me more,

like the saddest sadness ever,
but cast in platinum
and encased in diamonds.

On Being Rendered Speechless

Picking up and dropping off passengers there
is prohibited by law, even when driving a Mercedes,

so we might as well stay right where we are,
entwined around each other, the bed squeaking

unintelligibly under us as we grunt and gasp,
just about to let go of our entire combined vocabularies,

and all without what the guardians of language
would consider an appropriate level of remorse.

A Simple Prayer

My mom went
into the hospital
13 years ago today
and never came out.

Lord, protect me,
so every morning
I can sit by the window
and start a poem.

There's a beauty
in inventing things
that serve no purpose.

Who Is a Righteous Man?

In Jewish tradition,
a righteous man is buried
with 144 prayer books
on top of his coffin.

When my Uncle Lou
was buried, they put
the books in cardboard boxes
labeled Kitchen Utensils.

Today, at a traffic light
on Mass Ave., a panhandler
in a filthy Patriots jersey
shuffled over to my car.

I didn't roll down the window.
I didn't acknowledge him.
I just stared straight ahead,
trying to will the light to change.

Statistic

A boy lies sprawled
by the edge of the road,

his chest torn open
by a chunk of shrapnel.

You could see his heart beating
if you bothered to look.

III

The Day's Residue

There were more mass shootings in 2019 than there were days in the year. That's just the kind of place this is, mostly navigable in daylight, but, after dark, a whole other thing. "What are those bonfires?" I asked the migrants working side by side in the fields. They were like "Yes, yes, yes." I'm just now finding my way. Meanwhile, Marlene is resting at home, drinking a beer with the dude that shot her (whose nickname is Rabbit). It has nothing to do with forgiveness. It's simply that one person in six has never heard of the Holocaust. Freud said dreams are the day's residue. I think of it sometimes when I see Nazis marching into Poland on the History Channel.

Half-Mumbled Sentences

Is this your career? Seriously? Get a real job! Writing postcards doesn't count. Anyone can do it. Only violence helps where violence rules. I can still see the bright crimson glow. We didn't know meat tenderizer and saliva remove bloodstains. That's part of the mystery. I mean, every revolution is a throw of the dice. Turn up the television. Those Buddhist monks protesting in half-mumbled sentences sound like they might be saying "kupkes kupkes"—words that have nothing to do with religion, but refer to the spot in a bullring where the bull makes his stand. It's a good start.

After the Bomb

A former beauty queen has been found in her bedroom—decapitated, limbless, a chainsaw nearby. The floor is littered with discarded gloves and face masks. On the wall, a decorative wooden sign says, "Breathe deeply and calmly." How do you do that? This might not be hell, but it definitely isn't heaven. We need a plan, an intervention, something. In Hiroshima, after the bomb, they piled the bodies in the swimming pool at the college and cremated them with scrap wood. The smell of smoke chokes us; the heat scorches our eyeballs. Sirens scream in the distance. Assume the monster is everywhere.

Only Beauty Survives

The king delighted in varying which crown he wore. One day he'd wear a crown of gold; the next, a crown of silver or of iron, or even a crown eccentrically fashioned from barbed wire. When he wore the latter, he was always surprised when blood ran in rivulets into his eyes. The queen, meanwhile, hated anyone who might be thought more beautiful than she was. She frequently sent assassins throughout the land to eliminate all possible rivals. That sound isn't thunder, people would say, but an assassin rapping on the door of a cottage until his knuckles are raw.

Life and Nothing But

The police nowadays consider gatherings of three or more people a riot. I try desperately to speak out, shriek like someone warning of an approaching fire, but can't because of a sudden terrifying lack of breath. All these events, crises, dramas, convulsions—literature pales by comparison. When I cross any border, there is always an uneasy moment when I feel myself automatically regarded as an enemy. We are surrounded by murderers like those jellyfish on the beach: children stab them with sticks without realizing they are living creatures. Life is nothing but being stabbed, knifed. We are the wound.

It's Not Me, It's You

You hear the thin cries of a drowning man. You notice that seemingly-innocent words like "today," "yesterday," and "tomorrow" have been censored. You pick quarrels with the baggers at grocery stores. You try but fail to ignore the prevalence of right-wing militias, foreign movies dubbed in English, shark sightings. You prefer baseball to football and a medically-induced coma to either. You wonder what it would be like to suffer a gunshot. You have a recurrent dream where you're lost in an old abandoned warehouse, usually with a friend you had growing up whose brother played Russian roulette one time too many.

Oh, Mercy

I board the subway at 72nd Street carrying a metal briefcase like the one that contains secret nuclear launch codes. A busker playing guitar at the far end of the car is trying to make up in enthusiasm what he lacks in formal training. He apparently adheres to Lou Reed's dictum: anything with more than three chords is jazz. The passengers ignore his musical pleas for attention. They nap. They text. They shed virus. When the train emerges for a moment above ground, the sky looks as if it's been digitally erased. There are colors in nature that birds can see, but humans can't.

Rotten Tomatoes

Reclusive billionaire Howard Hughes watched his favorite movie, *Ice Station Zebra* (43% on Rotten Tomatoes), over and over for years on end. Flying insects embedded themselves in his skin. A nurse said in a calm voice, "It's all right," but something was wrong. He was drooling and thrashing his legs and reaching out. When the bed was transformed into a rectangle of sunlight, he was compelled to lie down, surrounded by stacks of untouched cash. If you want reality, go and stand there. You'll see it; it's there with the radio playing songs in the background about love's bloody thorns.

Eve of the Eve of Destruction

It was like my legs had carried me there by mistake. The police were throwing dissenters off roofs, out windows, from speeding cars. I'm sure there were many more under the mud. The little black dots I'd seen in the distance turned out to be the farmer's wife beating a tramp with a garden hoe. I didn't expect that, or that sirens would be wailing and dictators humping dead boys. One person in six hadn't heard yet, didn't know what it was: a planet of funeral homes and cemeteries.

Heart on Ice

I was driving like I always do—as if transporting a heart packed in ice for a patient in imminent danger of dying—when, outside Springfield, a bird that was also in an exceptional hurry crashed into my windshield with the boom of a gunshot, startling me about as bad as I've ever been startled, but the strangest part was that there were no cracks in the glass, no blood splatter, no feathers caught in the wipers, nothing, just the greasy crayon colors of dusk smeared all around, and the cold stretch of road ahead.

After Auschwitz

To write poetry after Auschwitz is barbaric.
—Theodor W. Adorno

All day and all night, the air is thick with smoke that smells like burning hair. The men in authority, when confronted, can't explain it. As a matter of fact, they don't even try; they just gesticulate in front of the cameras. You live in fear of losing a crap job and never finding another nearly as good. I'm watching an emerald-throated hummingbird at the feeder so I don't have to deal with all the bullshit. I don't want to make this sound worse than it is, but there isn't a lot else happening—just these assorted crises, each at a different point of unfolding. It's an intricate universe. Heartache is everybody's neighbor.

The Ladder

There are days when I look up from some small task—answering a text or fixing coffee or leashing the dog—and see miles more of the skyline burning and crowds chanting encouragement to the flames. On those days, I feel broken and hollow and lost—too old and slow to be able to make any sort of difference. Then I remember I don't have to be one of the ones who climb a rescue ladder; I can stand on the ground and help hold the ladder steady.

Apathy for the Devil

This is the country you heard rumors about: where the sky acquires the greenish sheen of sickness and birds are forced by the diseased air to fly close to the ground; where memory lasts just a very short time; where school hallways are spotted with blood and the cops have a penchant for suicide; where deranged angels hoot all night in the tree outside your window; where thought is folly, and endings go spectacularly wrong; where love, invisible until now but always there, spreads like a spider crack.

Birth, Death, Etc.

Somewhere I have a picture postcard of Kafka's birthplace in Prague. Even the cashiers at the gift shop there were imbued with a kind of perverted charm, offering suggestions about how to be productive while extremely depressed. Linger someplace too long, though, and the infrastructure starts to crumble. I was an adult when I realized there's no word that designates a person as being a parent who has lost a child—a word like "widow" or "orphan." Sartre's last words were, "I failed." Flags were burned in protest. The rest just flung flowers.

Threatened Birds Nesting

You're eating lunch on a bench in the park, close to a roped-off area where a sign says threatened birds are nesting. It's the first nice day in a week. You're enjoying the spring-like weather when a man you've never seen before steps out from behind a tree. He points a .38 special at you, shouts, "I regard Henry Ford as an inspiration," and fires. Within just hours, friends assemble a pop-up shrine at the spot with flowers, teddy bears, messages of love and respect. Not me—I'm reading true crime books in order to gather survival tips.

Pandemic

One day it's my 33-year-old cousin found dead in bed from an overdose; another day, it's high school seniors raising their arms in the Nazi salute for a yearbook photo; another, it's government protesters washing with bottles of Coke to help minimize the sting of tear gas. No place seems any realer than any other. A man in Warrenton, Missouri films himself licking deodorant sticks at a Walmart and asking, "Who's scared of coronavirus now?" Very soon, Jesus, looking extremely sharp in a dark gray funeral suit and standing behind the KFC, could be handing out tickets to heaven.

Connotations of Ancestral Home

I felt like I was on a bridge, and there were two or three heavy trucks, and the bridge was rocking—but there were no trucks. Even the dairy cows wondered what the fuck. At one point we seemed to be following Beethoven's footsteps through Vienna. This was someone's idea of paradise. It just wasn't mine. I wore only a sports jacket and shoes, no shirt or pants. The local women said that, when the time came, they wanted to be buried in their wedding dresses. They would later tell us many other disturbing things as machine

After the Plague

I'll step into the cold of new geometries—long stretches of emptiness bequeathed by tens of thousands of unnecessary deaths. There'll be decaying leaves scattered on the floor like notes from the kingdom of the sick, and the radio will play party songs from the sixties that, after our months of listening to liars, will sound unintelligible. I'll feel rather than see the close proximity of broken oaths and blood debts. All around us, the world will gratefully resume its ritual practices, preferring old familiar crimes to novel diseases. Night will end, only to begin again—a great black coffin.

Epistemologies of Ignorance

A World War I Zeppelin floats above. It's the kind of shit that wears me down. What year was it they took our memories and replaced them with canisters of decaying film? Lately, I've collected inspiration on my walks—cocoons and nests and thorns—and pinned them to the wall. A tabby cat like the one Picasso gave his mistress when her dog disappeared in 1945 is last on the list. They say a man is a wolf to his fellow man. Bob from next door waves hello regardless; it gives him something to do with his hands.

The End of Nature

I fell asleep to the rat-tat-tat of rain and dreamed I could breathe underwater. The grieving came later, when they cut open the belly of a stranded whale and found coins and plastic water bottles inside. Then I learned there could be such a thing as too much sun. Now I'm wondering what comes next—if we'll only be able to view nature in assigned locations. You'll go and sit in a darkened theater, surrounded by dozens of strangers, and when you start to sob, not even half the people there will understand.

Anniversary

Every time is the first time our bodies are steeped in each other—why there are yellow birds singing in my chest, heatwaves and widespread wildfires, the three laws of thermodynamics temporarily suspended as windows fill, ipso facto, with silver; nowhere else for the rainy day kind of light to go; a room that changes shape like a cloud; witches and saints, arms linked, dancing in a circle around the bed, their robes lying in a heap on the floor; our disorderliness the order of the day; blowing up the paper bag and hitting it so it pops.

Oracle

A woman named for a dead grandmother crossed her arms across her chest in a conscious attempt to hide her trembling. She thought the birds up in the trees sounded like they were asking, "Hey, you all right?" Most of her communications with the world were strained or superficial. It took a while before she realized that everything she was interested in saying was contained somewhere in a book. Now when she closes her eyes, she can see flowers, fire creatures, viruses leaping from the cracked tarmac. She hesitates to call them visitors. More like, chasing pink, she found red.

Flight into Darkness

I seem to have discovered my shadow side—a wardrobe with mystery contents, blue and purple and full of leprous spots. Which isn't to say I feel sad or lonely. Rather, I'm noticing different details. The world right now, mostly it's news of the virus. We first heard the rumors from travelers. Men: quiet, faces drawn; women: often sobbing. We didn't believe them. The weather was just too beautiful. We lazed around, eating cherries, one basket after another, and ignored the elderly stumbling down the road from time to time, buckling under their loads.

Sick World

A usually-bustling city is eerily vacant. Essential supplies now include liquor, guns, and toilet paper. Who isn't secretly embarrassed? Around midnight I take a puzzle apart just for the hell of it. The next morning my department holds a Zoom session on how to prevent cheating in online classes. Other professors mention they also have been having strange dreams. In mine, I'm eating Crown Fried Chicken on a bench while eyeballs the size of boulders roll across the grass and dirt and a woman I recognize from TV weeps into her hands.

Between Life and Death

We're always evolving, always about to become something else, always both here and not here. Punk musicians who overdosed in flophouses, and child refugees who died in the camps, and American soldiers killed in Iraq pass each other on the worm-eaten stairs. Maybe if I walk really, really carefully, I can escape notice. People are acting more than just a little crazy. I can't see from this distance who that is writhing on the ground, but whoever it is, they're beating him to death with baseball bats. A woman keeps screaming, "No! No!" God is a joke that nobody gets.

The Endless Inventory of Human Cruelty

In general, it isn't good to be too close to all the passersby. I wonder what their breath will morph into next, or if it'll just disappear. Every morning of late, I've been writing down my dreams at the dining room table, employing a unique alphabet I created, scribbles formed by my non-dominant hand. The dreams can be distressingly real—a skull caved in with a brick, a dog set on fire, Jews hanged from lampposts, a mother raped in front of her children. Sometimes I start to sob so loud that everyone else stops yelling and stares at me.

Stick Figure Family

My father was a mass shooter—metaphorically speaking, of course—and my mother, a suicide bomber in a dynamite vest. God, the things I saw! Shattered arms, legs, heads. If it wasn't for lack of encouragement growing up, I might have become an avant-garde artist, someone famous for his controversial stick figures drawn on toilet paper. Instead, I keep my face blank, even when a family is seized on the street and dragged away. Everything seems to stop abruptly to consider what just happened and then, as abruptly, resume, like a self-driving Mercedes that sacrifices pedestrians to save the driver.

Failed Poet Theater

You had never taken hallucinogens before. When you came back, you tried telling me that a word is many things, and it's the sum of the many things, and it's also not the many things combined. If the word is "beauty," for example, it can become "beautiful." Then it can become "beauteous" or "beautification." All this time, a ratty top hat was balanced on your head at a treacherous angle. I just sat in the window—10, 20 minutes—just sat in silence, as if watching out for a black man running down the street in fear for his life.

Anger Is an Arrow

The sun was shining for once, and I was sitting out on the patio with a book—Clare Carlisle's *Philosopher of the Heart: The Restless Life of Soren Kierkegaard*—open on my lap, while I stared off into the middle distance, trying to think of a specific skill my angry, beautiful, workaholic father had taught me growing up—how to change the oil in a car, for example, or restring a steel-string acoustic guitar, or make sourdough starter from scratch—and I couldn't. I couldn't think of one. Unless, that is, you consider being a yellow bull's-eye a skill.

Mood Pill

Per doctor's instructions, I take the pill as needed, which can mean three, four, even five times each day. I do what I must—a dog obsessively licking its sore parts. When I was growing up, my mother used to collect Green Stamps. It promised utopia, but it could be hell. She would exchange them at the store for oven mitts or a toaster. All these years later, only burned trees are left. A heat ray designed by the military makes asylum seekers feel like their skin is on fire as soon as they get within sight of the border.

For Those Who Are Ignorant of History

The smoke that was billowing from the big building with a wide chimney and fifteen ovens had once been women and children. The bodies. The hair. The fingernails. Everything. No one asked how they were killed, though the crickets did begin chirping, thinking it was night. How will we ever get out of this labyrinth? What's a conspiracy theory today will be policy tomorrow. The brain likes crazy. We have to learn to live with it. The first step is to acknowledge that fire is inevitable. You can't believe how fast those embers fly at you.

Do the Paranoid Style

Everything is either too hot or too cold, and nothing is soft. People are afraid of kissing, touching, being in a crowd. The ancient Chinese would carry lanterns lit by fireflies when passing through the streets at night. I have spent many nights these past six months watching out the window for the infected monkeys that are supposedly crossing the Atlantic on rafts of vegetation. A military gas mask hangs from a hook on the back of the door just in case. I don't know how I know, but I know that a group of sharks is called a shiver.

Gunmetal Sky

Dying on your birthday would be the ultimate irony, so we'll avoid street corner gatherings, malls, Purim parties, even poetry that sounds like it was written by someone who would lick a toilet seat on a bet. In fact, we won't be going anywhere for a while now that a microsecond can last forever if the destroying angel, lurid teeth bared, thrusts its face perilously close to yours.

&

There aren't enough police to patrol the city, or enough soldiers to defend it, or enough doctors and nurses to heal the sick. The angel goes raging across a gunmetal sky, and—be-bop-a-lula—an inmate hangs himself in his cell with an extension cord, and a 3-year-old drowns at the edge of the sea, and a dump truck packed with corpses backs up to a burial trench.

&

What I had assumed last night was the crackle of firecrackers may have been a gun going off. Don't go back to sleep. A full clip holds thirty bullets.

&

Just a few months ago, this condition had no name; now there are special news reports about it. People watching think, "Close the borders!" Today, despite the situation all over the world, raindrops shake the glass, making beautiful drip paintings on windows.

Acknowledgements & Citations

The author wishes to thank the editors of the following journals in which some of the poems in this volume originally appeared, occasionally in somewhat different form: *Thimble Literary Magazine*; *Live Nude Poems*; *Microfiction Monday*; *The Big Windows Review: Isacoustic*; *Dodging the Rain*; *Boston Literary Magazine: The Voices Project*; *A Story in 100 Words: Red Eft Review*; *Biscuit Root Drive*; *Impaired*; *All the Sins*; *misery tourism*; *What Rough Beast; former people*; *City. River. Tree.*; *Club Plum*; *One Sentence Poems*; *right hand pointing*; *The Daily Drunk*; *Beatnik Cowboy*; and *As It Ought to Be*.

"The Gray Man" was inspired by this article: http://idiommag.com/2012/10/the-handmade-luther-price

"The Third Reich of Dreams" was inspired by these articles: https://neglectedbooks.com/?p=4797 & https://www.newyorker.com/books/second-read/how-dreams-change-under-authoritarianism

"Holocaust Train" is a found poem derived from this article: https://www.npr.org/2020/01/27/798480937/75-years-after-auschwitz-liberation-survivors-urge-world-to-remember

About the Author

Howie Good, Ph.D., a journalism professor at SUNY New Paltz, is the winner of the 2019 Grey Book Press Chapbook Competition for *What It Is and How to Use It*, the 2017 Lorien Poetry Prize from Thoughtcrime Press for *The Loser's Guide to Street Fighting*, and the 2015 Press Americana Prize for Poetry for *Dangerous Acts Starring Unstable Elements*. His other books include *The Death Row Shuffle* (Finishing Line Press, 2020) and *The Trouble with Being Born* (Ethel Micro Press, 2020).

www.ingramcontent.com/pod-product-compliance
Lightning Source LLC
Chambersburg PA
CBHW070122110526
44587CB00017BA/3238